SAYING NO TO NICK

Vicki Coghill
Craig Longmuir

RISING STARS

First published in the UK by
Rising Stars UK Ltd.
7 Hatchers Mews, Bermondsey Street, London SE1 3GS
www.risingstars-uk.com

This edition published 2011
Reprinted 2014

Text © UC Publishing Pty Ltd.
www.ucpublishing.com

First published 2006 by Insight Publications Pty Ltd.
ABN 57 005 102 983,
89 Wellington Street,
St Kilda, Victoria 3182
Australia

Development: UC Publishing Pty Ltd
Cover design: UC Publishing/Design Ed
Written by: Vicki Coghill
Illustrations: Craig Longmuir
Text design and typesetting: Design Ed/Clive Sutherland
Editorial consultancy: Dee Reid

British Library Cataloguing in Publication Data.
A CIP record for this book is available from the British Library.

ISBN: 978-1-84680-810-4

Printed by Craft Print International Ltd., Singapore

Contents

Characters

Dave

Benny

Will

Nick

Chapter 1
Meet Nick Zanetti

Nick Zanetti is about the coolest kid in the whole school. Every kid wants to be his friend, and every girl wants to be his girl. Even new kids to the school, like me, are quickly told about Nick Zanetti.

I remember my first day at this school.

'Hi, Dave, welcome to our school. You'll be in 7B. A nice class. Nick Zanetti is in 7B,' said the head teacher.

'Nick who?' I thought.

'We'll sit you near Nick,' said my class teacher. 'That way Nick will be there to help you.'

I couldn't believe it. Who *was* this guy?

It's as if people just fall all over him trying to get on his good side. Even some of the teachers seem to give Nick special treatment.

'Would you like a chocolate, Nick?'

'Can I get you something from the shop, Nick?'

'Didn't finish your homework, Nick? Just get it in tomorrow.'

Some nights I go to bed and dream about what it must be like to be Nick Zanetti.

But every morning I wake up and I'm still me, plain old Dave Ling. Ordinary-looking, with long, lanky arms and legs. Especially when there are girls around! The only girl that ever shows any interest in me is my dog, Jess.

The one thing I have in common with Nick Zanetti is football. We're in the same team. He's the star striker in the Woodley Comets but I'm only the goalie. I may as well be invisible to Nick and the rest of his gang.

On Monday nights, I go to training and run a few laps. I take a few knocks and bumps from Nick and his best friend, Will. They are always pushing past me to get to the drinks or talk to the coach.

After training, my mum picks me up or I walk home with Ben Murphy. Benny lives in the same street as me. He's a nice guy but he's a little weird. His mum makes him play football. She hopes that he'll develop some interest in sports. Benny is *really* into computers and electrical stuff. He likes to take things apart and put them back together in different ways. Some of his inventions are pretty interesting. However, it's not the type of stuff that'll get you in with the cool crowd.

Benny's a bit of a drag sometimes. He's always trying to talk to me about his latest gizmo. I'd rather just watch what basketball tricks Nick and the others are doing. It must be so cool to be Nick Zanetti.

Chapter 2
The game

On Saturday morning, we have a football match. Mum drops Benny and me around the corner from the football ground. That way, I can walk in without the other guys seeing my mum drop me off. It's not cool to be seen with your mum. I drag my old bike out of the boot of the car! I have to ride home tonight as Mum can't pick me up.

Nick and the rest of his gang race in through the gates on shiny new bikes. They skid to a stop in a spray of gravel and throw their bikes onto the ground. I had to do odd jobs for months to save enough to buy my second-hand bike. 'If I owned a bike like that,' I think, 'I'd treat it much better.'

The game that day against the Henley
Rovers is really tough. Even Nick Zanetti
is finding the going hard. The Rovers keep
blocking his passes and bring the ball zooming
down towards the goal. Benny is no use to
anyone. He just gets in our way.

Then Nick trips Benny up on the way past. He laughs as Benny falls face down in the dirt.

'At least you might actually block the ball down there, Murphy!' laughs Nick.

I manage to make some really good saves but a couple of goals sneak through. Then Nick scores the winning goal. Everybody cheers, as usual.

As we walk to the gate, Nick slaps me on the back. 'Good game, Ling! Want to come with us to Mario's for pizza?' he says.

My whole chest feels as if it's going to explode. I just manage to stutter 'Y-yeah, sure!' before we're on our bikes.

I can see Benny standing quietly at the gate, waiting for me. I don't look at him as I race past him and set off for Mario's.

Chapter 3
Hanging out with Nick

After that, it's as if my whole life gets that little bit better. I'm not part of the real 'in' group but I'm close enough. I get to sit with Nick Zanetti and his crowd at school and I get to hang out with them after school.

It feels pretty good to have the other kids at school look up to you as you walk past. I know they're wishing that they could hang out with Nick Zanetti too.

The only problem is Benny. He comes up to me when I'm with Nick and tries to tell me things about his latest stupid invention. It's really embarrassing.

Nick looks cross when Benny walks over to the gang. I know that Nick regrets letting me hang out with his gang. So I turn my back on Benny and freeze him out.

Then, one Thursday night after school, something happens. I'm standing around with Nick, Will and the guys when Benny walks past. He is carrying a pile of electrical stuff.

Nick looks quickly at me, then sticks his foot out in front of Benny. He sends him flying to the ground.

'Oh, looks like poor Benny tripped over,' says Nick.

Benny picks up the smashed circuit boards and valves. His knees are cut and I can see blood on his fingers. Some of the glass bits have cut him.

Benny looks at me as he hurries past. But I can't meet his eyes.

Since then, Nick is always trying to get
Benny. He goes out of his way to catch Benny
on his way home, in the school playground, in
the park. He always finds some way to put him
down or hurt him in front of others.

It's as if being mean to Benny makes Nick feel good. When everybody is laughing at the things he says to Benny, Nick gets this really smug look on his face. That look is really starting to get to me.

Chapter 4
Time to say no

'Mrs Murphy came to see me today, David,' says Mum. She stops stirring the pan on the stove and wipes her hand across her brow.

'She says that she thinks Benny is being bullied but he won't tell her anything. He has bruises. His clothes are always getting torn and lots of his things seem to turn up broken. You don't know anything about it, do you, David?'

I mutter something, not daring to speak. I can feel the flush spreading up my neck to the tips of my ears. Mum is too busy stirring the chilli to notice.

'I don't know how people can just stand around and watch stuff like this happen. Somebody must see what's going on. I guess nobody is brave enough to stand up for Benny.'

Suddenly, I'm not hungry anymore.

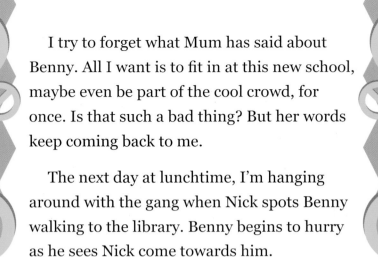

I try to forget what Mum has said about Benny. All I want is to fit in at this new school, maybe even be part of the cool crowd, for once. Is that such a bad thing? But her words keep coming back to me.

The next day at lunchtime, I'm hanging around with the gang when Nick spots Benny walking to the library. Benny begins to hurry as he sees Nick come towards him.

'Where do you think you're going, Benny?' asks Nick. The other kids circle around Benny.

'Uh, n-nowhere, Nick,' Benny stammers.

'Come and play ball with us, Benny,' says Nick. He drags Benny towards the library wall. Benny lets himself be pulled along until he finds himself pushed against the wall. The members of Nick's gang surround him.

Nick stands, legs braced. He throws a basketball from hand to hand. Suddenly, he hurls it at Benny's face. It smashes into Benny's nose, which begins to bleed. Tears stream down his face. He tries to stop the blood spattering onto his clothes.

Suddenly a voice rings out.

'NO! THAT'S ENOUGH!' Before I realise it is me, I step in between Nick and Benny.

Nick looks at me hard.

'You're making a mistake, Ling!'

'No I'm not Nick. I'm not going to let you beat up my friend!'

There is a moment's silence. I stare into Nick's eyes. He stares back at me. I start to sweat. I brace myself for the fist I am sure is coming.

Suddenly, Nick shrugs and turns away.

'They're not worth it. Come on, guys. Let's go.'

Some of Nick's gang turn to follow. Will hesitates, then walks over to Benny and me. He picks up Benny's books and hands them to him.

'How's the nose?' he asks Benny. He gives me a grin. 'What you did just now—that took guts. You're OK.'

Chapter 5
New friends

It's pretty interesting at school now. Benny, Will and I still play football, but we've joined the Science Club as well. We're planning to build some amazing stuff. In fact, I'm on my way home now to do some work on our latest project.

There's this girl, too—Sarah. She's kind of been looking a bit interested in me since the day I said no to Nick Zanetti. She's really pretty. I wouldn't have had the guts to even talk to her before. I can't stop thinking about her.

I'm thinking about asking her to go to see a film. But it's hard to get those words out when she's standing with all her friends.
Maybe I can call her mobile.

I'm still thinking about Sarah when I hear a yell behind me. A quick look back and I'm on the move. But not fast enough. Nick Zanetti and two of his gang are heading straight for me. Are they trying to run me down? Suddenly, Benny appears out of nowhere on his bike. He skids to a stop directly between me and the oncoming bikes. 'Benny!' I yell.

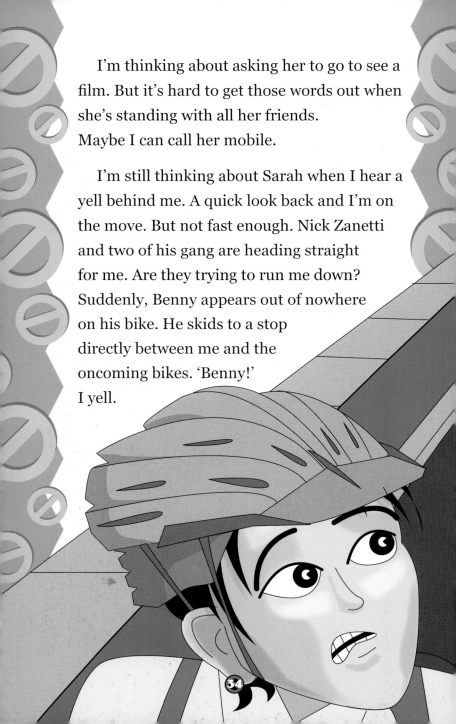

The bikes race straight at Benny. I stand frozen, watching them getting nearer. When they reach Benny, one of them hits his front wheel, tipping him over. The others swerve around Benny and are upon me.

I twist to one side and leap out of the way. I come down heavily. I can hear them laughing as they race past me.

There's a terrible pain in my leg and my head spins. I'm going to need help and soon. I look up and see Benny standing over me.

'You'll be OK,' he says. I try to get up but the pain in my leg screams at me.

'It could be broken,' says Benny. 'Stay still. I'll go and get help.'

I sit still, holding my leg. I watch out for Zanetti's gang to come back. But mainly I think about how brave Benny had been.

The accident when I broke my leg was at the end of last year. I was in plaster for most of the holidays, but Benny came to my place every day to play computer games. We got really good at Alien Wars. Now Benny and I have plans for great stuff with soldering irons and electrical equipment. This is going to be a good year. Who cares about Nick Zanetti?